# CHILDREN'S FIRST BOOK OF CHESS

CHILDREN'S FIRST BOOK OF CHESS

by Natalie Shevando and Matthew McMillion

Illustrations by Andrii Dankovych

Interior book design by Max Mendor

© 2021, Natalie Shevando

Illustrations © 2021, Natalie Shevando

Publishers Maxim Hodak & Max Mendor

© 2021, Glagoslav Publications

www.glagoslav.com

ISBN: 978-1-914337-24-6

First published by Glagoslav Publications in November 2021

A catalogue record for this book is available from the British Library.

This book is in copyright. No part of this publication may be reproduced, stored in a retrieval system or transmitted in any form or by any means without the prior permission in writing of the publisher, nor be otherwise circulated in any form of binding or cover other than that in which it is published without a similar condition, including this condition, being imposed on the subsequent purchaser.

NATALIE SHEVANDO   MATTHEW McMILLION

# CHILDREN'S FIRST BOOK OF CHESS

GLAGOSLAV PUBLICATIONS

Dear Children,
Please enjoy this delightful book with beautiful illustrations! I do hope that through this book, you'll fall in love with chess and it will bring you many wonderful moments in your life. Enjoy!

— Boris Gelfand,
Vice World Chess Champion.

# Contents

Introduction . . . . . . . . . . . . . . . . . . . . . . . . . . . 7
1. How chess came to life . . . . . . . . . . . . . . . . . . . 9
2. When chess brought peace to the land . . . . . . . 11
3. How chess spread around the world,
   and even to Harry Potter! . . . . . . . . . . . . . . . . .13
4. Chess in action: the gameplay and more . . . . . .16
5. A few words about how chess is played today . . . 19
6. And what about the chessboard? . . . . . . . . . . .21
7. From humble pawn to mighty king:
   all the pieces, one by one . . . . . . . . . . . . . . . . 24
8. Your queen is highly valuable,
   but your king is priceless . . . . . . . . . . . . . . . . 38
9. The three stages of every chess game . . . . . . . .41
10. Don't forget these simple rules . . . . . . . . . . . 44
11. Want to be a chess grandmaster?
    Start playing when you're a kid! . . . . . . . . . . 46
12. Chess even has a few relatives around the world . . 48
13. Playing chess in outer space? That's right! . . . . 52
14. What about playing chess underwater? . . . . . . 54
15. Welcome to Chess Village,
    where kids can be game pieces! . . . . . . . . . . 56
16. Making chess part of your life: for fun,
    family, and a sharper mind . . . . . . . . . . . . . 59
17. World Chess Champions . . . . . . . . . . . . . . . .61
18. About the Authors . . . . . . . . . . . . . . . . . . . 62

# Introduction

Chess is truly an extraordinary game.

Today more than 600 million people around the world regularly play chess, and that number gets bigger every year! Why is it so well loved?

The book you have in front of you will answer this question, and you will also learn many fascinating facts about chess and its long history.

Read on and find out how chess first appeared, and how it changed over time. You will get to know each chess piece, one by one, and understand the idea behind the game, what it's really all about. You will learn about the chessboard, chess rules and tournaments, as well as other games related to chess. We will also share with you some interesting facts about chess life.

Chess is certainly a brilliant and beneficial game. It gradually sharpens your mind while fine-tuning your character.

# 1. How chess came to life

Ancient legends tell us that Chaturanga, a game played by two or four people, is the game that started it all. It is the earliest version of our modern game of chess. But this is only one of several legends. In fact, there are a few different stories about how chess came to be.

Here's the most famous of them all: once upon a time, 2000 years ago, India was ruled by the mighty King Bagram. He had a massive army of one hundred thousand foot soldiers, plus thirty thousand battle horses and elephants. The king crushed all his enemies, until finally there was no one left to fight. So, the bored king commanded his people to come up with a new kind of entertainment.

One wise man brought him a board and a set of wooden pieces. When the king gazed upon them, he saw his entire army right in front of him: all the horses, the foot soldiers, the generals, and even himself. On one side of the board, the wise man set up the white king's army, and on the opposite side, he placed the black king's forces.

The king loved the game so much that he decided to reward the old man with gold. But the wise man said he would rather have wheat than gold. He asked the king to place one grain of wheat on the first square of the chessboard, and then double the number of grains for each additional square, one after the other, all the way up to the 64$^{th}$ square. This seemed like a bargain for the king, at first.

But before long, the king understood that this would be more wheat than you could find in the entire world! In fact, if you could somehow gather up all this wheat, the pile would be taller than Mount Everest itself! So, that day, the wise man showed the king some of the mystery and power of chess.

# 2. WHEN CHESS BROUGHT PEACE TO THE LAND

Another Indian legend says that once there lived a king who had twin sons. One wore black, while the other wore white, and this was the only difference between them. Then one day, their old father died, leaving one half of the country to each of his two sons. But both of these new kings wanted to rule the entire country all for himself, and so they started a war. The war was long and many lives were lost.

The people found a wise man to go and speak with the kings. He told the two brothers that he could show them a peaceful way to end the war. They both agreed to see what he could share with them. So, the wise man carried in a wooden board, set it down, and placed upon it small, carved pieces that symbolized the twins in white and black clothes.

The brother in white was the winner of the game. He then became the King of India and led his country to prosperity. After that, everyone in the land started playing chess, because it was the game that had finally brought peace to the country. And to commemorate that great victory, from that day on, the white pieces always move first.

# 3. How chess spread around the world, and even to Harry Potter!

Chess began its triumphant march around the world. The rules, the board and the pieces went through various changes over time. On his chessboard, the Turco-Mongolian conqueror Tamerlane played with such pieces as the camel, the giraffe, the siege engine, and even the crocodile. In Persia, the game was used for training military commanders. The Arabs conquered Persia and helped spread chess to other countries.

During the 8th-9th centuries, via the Arabs, the game reached Spain. After another couple of centuries, it became well-known in Portugal, Italy, and France. By the 11th century, chess was known all over Europe and Scandinavia, and finally, all around the world. What's even more interesting is that a chess book was the second book ever printed in the English language.

The Catholic Church used to forbid chess, because they considered it to be gambling. Decrees against chess were issued by King Henry III of England and King Louis IX of France, but the game outlived all of them. But Louis XIV, also known

as the "Sun King," was a great fan of chess. During his reign, his entire royal household started playing chess.

The oldest chess pieces that have survived to this day are Lewis chessmen, named after the Isle of Lewis in Scotland, where they were discovered in the year 1831. They were carved out of walrus ivory and whale teeth way back in the 12th century! These ancient pieces were the inspiration for Wizard's Chess in the film *Harry Potter and the Philosopher's Stone.*

# 4. Chess in action: the gameplay and more

It took many years before chess became the game that we know today. The modern rules of the game were established in the 18<sup>th</sup> century and have not changed since then.

Today, chess is played all over the world! But why do so many people enjoy moving pieces across the game's black-and-white checkered board? It is not simply about winning. Rather, because chess makes you smarter, by training your mind and your memory.

Tests have shown that the IQs of great chess players are among the highest in the world!

On top of that, chess teaches us how to think out-of-the-box, to plan our next moves, and to make the best decisions while the clock is ticking. It teaches us how to win with respect, and how to lose with honor. Chess combines art, science, and sport, and everyone can find something special in it.

Currently, every year, on the 20th of July, International Chess Day is celebrated in 195 countries around the world.

This day commemorates the establishment of FIDE, the International Chess Federation. The organization was founded back in 1924, and then 42 years later, July 20th became the day when millions of chess players from East to West celebrate their favorite game.

# 5. A FEW WORDS ABOUT HOW CHESS IS PLAYED TODAY

What is chess like today? It is a competitive, logical board game for two players. You play it on a 64-square board with special game pieces. Each turn, you can move one of your pieces and possibly capture (take) one of the pieces of your opponent. When you take one of your opponent's pieces, you move the captured piece away from the board, and replace it with your piece on the same square.

To make sure that chess players do not spend too much time thinking their moves over, a chess clock is used. It was designed in the 19th century by the engineer Thomas B. Wilson. Without the clock, some games could go on and on for many hours or even days. At one international tournament, a chess match did not finish, because both players fell asleep. Before the mechanical clock was invented, a sand hourglass was used.

All the moves of a chess game are recorded using a special set of descriptive terms called chess notation. The game ends when one player wins. And, of course, both players may finally agree to call the game "a draw," which means there is no winner and no loser, if neither player sees a way to win.

# 6. And what about the chessboard?

The black-and-white battlefield of chess is what we call a chessboard. On the chessboard, you can see 64 squares: 32 white and 32 black. The black and white colors alternate, and at first you might think that you can position the board any way you want. But this is not true. Before starting to play, make sure that the left corner square closest to you is black. On the edges of the board, the files (vertical lines) are marked with letters (a, b, c, d, e, f, g, h), and the ranks (horizontal lines) are marked with numbers (1 to 8). This will help you identify the needed square easier.

So, the rows of squares opposite to the numbers are the horizontal ranks. And the columns of squares on the other side of the letters are the vertical files. Therefore, every square belongs to one rank and one file and has a name or coordinates. For example, the square on file f and rank 4 is square f4.

For a very long time, chessboards did not all look alike. They could be tiny or huge, shaped like a triangle or even a hexagon! Today's chessboard is square and compact (with a side length of about 50 cm). For convenience, many of them

fold in half, making it possible for the chess pieces to be stored within the underside of the chessboard.

The first folding chessboard was made by one creative priest during the 12th century. The church did not approve of the game, so he came up with a clever little trick: the folded chessboard looked like books stacked on top of one another.

Such a variety of colors were used to decorate these early chessboards! Sometimes blue and red or yellow with green were the colors of choice. Rich players loved to play on boards painted gold and silver. In the East, the board was commonly white, with lines defining the squares.

Nowadays, the squares on the boards are usually yellow and brown, even though people call them "black and white." The reason for this is so that players can more easily keep track of their pieces on the board and plan their next moves across the squares.

# 7. From Humble Pawn to Mighty King: All the Pieces, One by One

And now let's get to know the different members of the chess army. There are 32 pieces in the game, 16 for each player: eight pawns, two knights, two bishops, two rooks, as well as one queen and one king, black and white. Let's see how they look and move.

**Pawns** look like soldiers with round helmets. During the Middle Ages, some players even gave each pawn its own name. For example, a merchant, a doctor, a weaver, or an innkeeper… But the tradition didn't last long. In several languages, the origin of the word "pawn" is related to the word for "foot soldier," and in other languages – to the word for "peasant."

François-André Danican Philidor, the greatest chess theorist of the 18th century, said: "The pawns are the soul of chess." The pawns are the first to attack and to be attacked. The first time a pawn moves, it may advance two squares if they are not occupied. The pawn attacks by moving forward diagonally one square to any side (Picture 1). Even though the pawn is the weakest piece, it can cause a big impact in the game.

If you move a pawn all the way to the opposite side of the board, this tiny but noble piece can be promoted to any other piece you would like, except for the king. When this happens, you simply take the pawn off the board and replace it with a new piece.

The pawn has an interesting way of attacking that is different from how it moves: it can capture, or "take" an enemy pawn that advances two squares from its initial position, if it passes over the attacked square. This is referred to as capturing a pawn "in passing" (en passant).

**Knight.** A knight in chess looks like a mighty horse's head. It is famous for its unique move: two squares forward and one to the side (Picture 2). The knight can move in any direction. Interestingly, only a knight can jump over other pieces (friend or foe) to reach its destination. By the way, this special ability of the knight brought about several colloquial expressions.

You can recognize the **bishop** by the piece's tall and tapered headdress. Just like the knight, the bishop belongs to the minor (light) pieces. However, the bishop is believed to be slightly stronger than the knight. A bishop can move diagonally with no restrictions in terms of distance or direction, but only if there are no other pieces standing in its way (Picture 3). A bishop cannot jump over them like the knight can.

**The rook** looks like the tower of a castle. It belongs to the major (heavy) pieces. In a fight, it can be compared to a cannon: it shoots hard and far. The rook moves vertically and horizontally in all directions, forwards and backwards, right and left, across any number of squares you would like (Picture 4).

**The queen** is an extremely important piece in chess. It has the power of the rook and the bishop to move vertically, horizontally, or diagonally (Picture 5). And it can also capture from any distance. Protect your queen: this major piece is the strongest on the board, both in attack and defense.

But the queen was not always so powerful. Initially, its only move was one square diagonally. It was like this up until the 15th century when Queen Isabella I of Castile became one of the greatest governors of Europe. A passionate chess player, she changed the rules so the queen would be the most powerful piece among all others on the board.

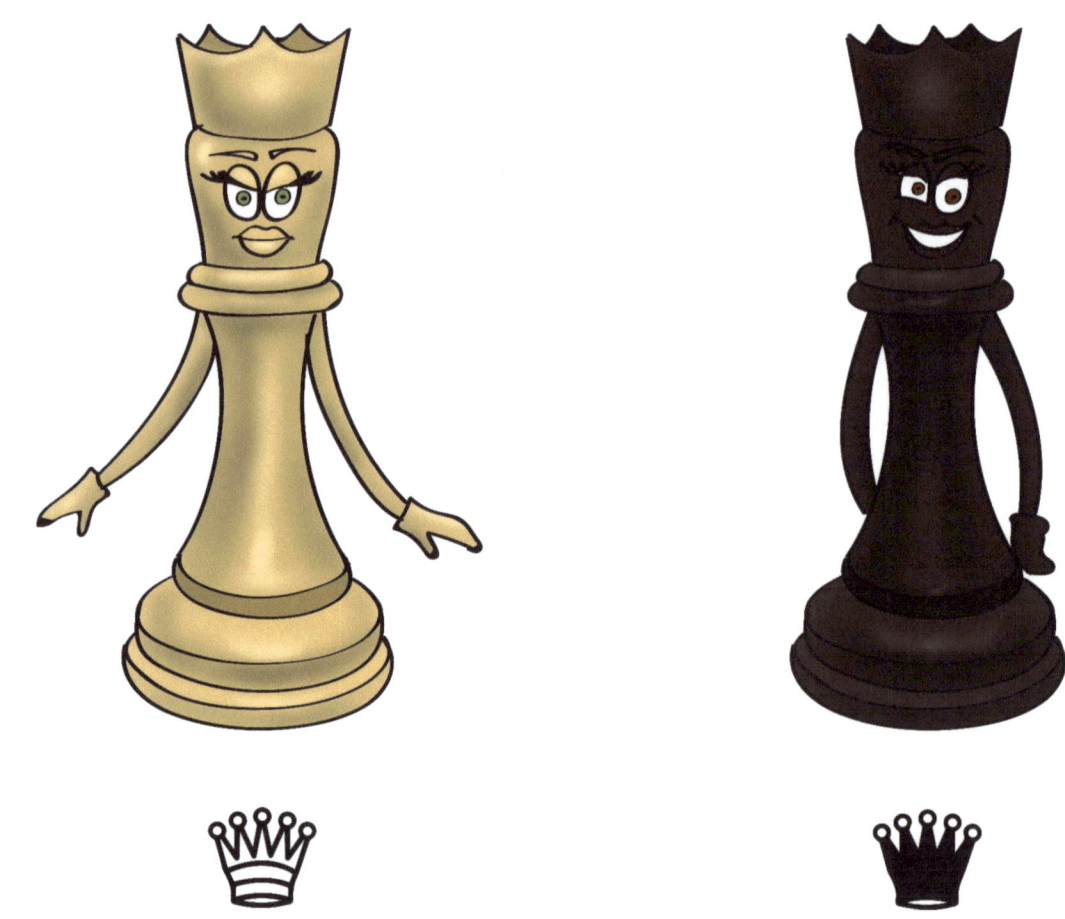

**The king** is the tallest of all the pieces on the chessboard. This magnificent piece appears to be a man wearing a tapered or cross-shaped crown. The king is the most important piece there is, one which the entire game is played around. The king can move in any direction, but only one square (Picture 6). You must always protect your king, because if he is defeated, this means the end of the game. But how can you protect your king from being attacked? By castling! This is a special move where the king "jumps over" one or two squares to the right or the left, while the rook shields it by standing on the square right next to it.

The goal of the game is clear: to get to the enemy king. This is how it usually happens: first, there will be check (which means the king is under immediate attack) and then checkmate, or mate (the end of the game). The one who defeats the other player's king is the winner. The terms check and mate originate from the Persian phrase shāh māt, which means the king is helpless.

Picture 1

Picture 2

Picture 3

Picture 4

Picture 5

Picture 6

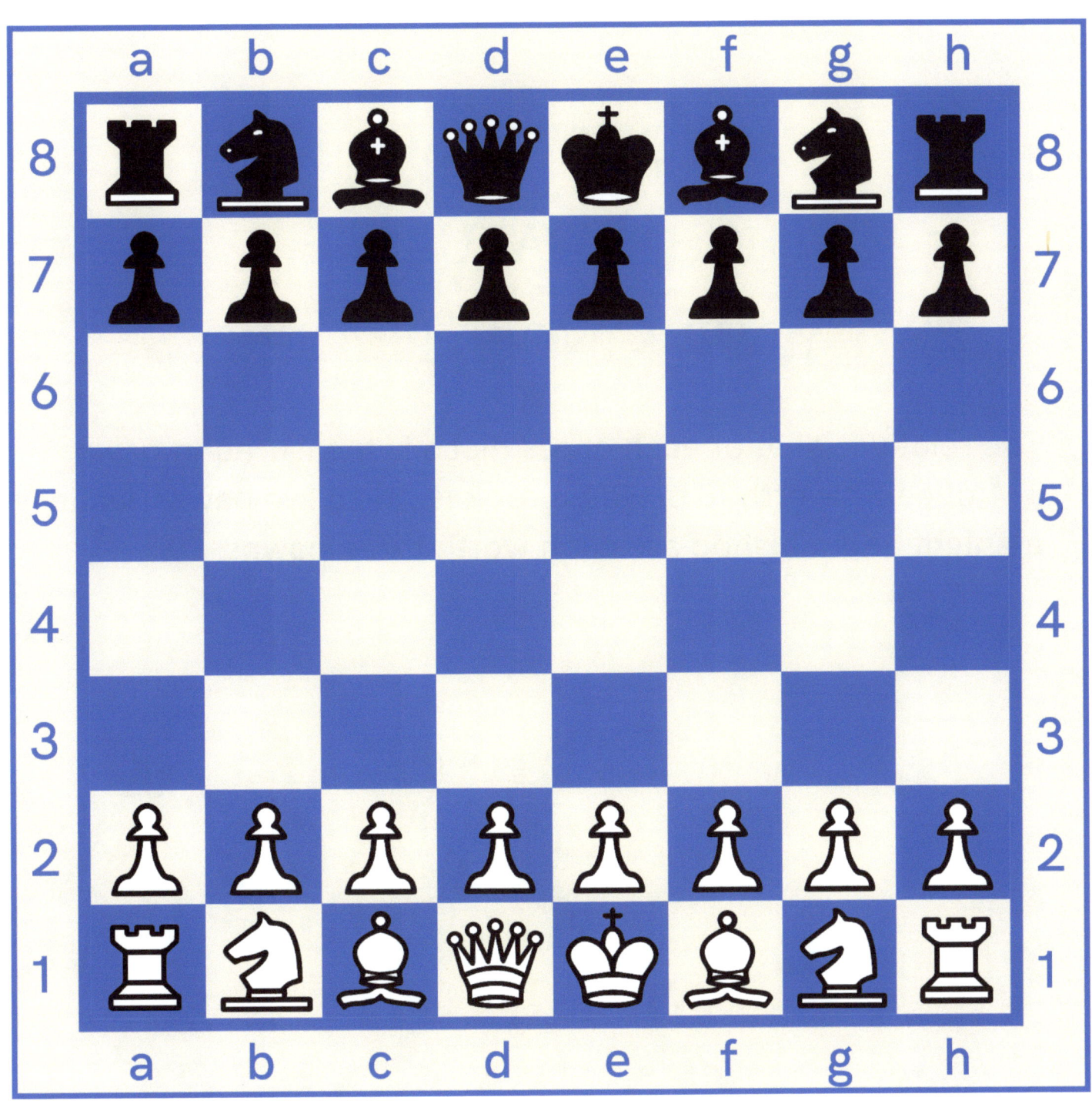

Chessboard Diagram

# 8.1 Your queen is highly valuable, but your king is priceless

The relative value of each chess piece is measured in pawns. A queen is worth 10 pawns, a rook is worth five pawns, while a knight and a bishop are each worth three pawns.

Since the king is the most important piece in the game, its value is not measured. Because if you lose the king, this means losing the entire game.

= PRICELESS

# 9. The three stages of every chess game

There are hundreds of ways to begin a chess game and thousands of choices after that. If you look at all the possibilities, the longest game could last for up to 5949 moves! There is no way anyone could keep all those combinations in mind! But there are some effective recommendations for players just starting out. The game has three parts, and there are a few helpful tips to share for each one of them.

**The opening** is the beginning. The first moves set the foundation for the entire game ahead. If most of your pieces stay where they are, it will be hard for you to win. Learn how to make the best choices for your pieces and predict the moves of your opponent. But remember: your opponent will always try to take control of the center. Place your major pieces there, and that means your queen, your knights, or your rooks. They are the ones who will carry you straight to victory.

**The middle game** is the main part of the game. This is where so much of the action happens. The pieces have taken up their strategic positions and are ready to battle. Each of the players has chosen their plans. Now everything depends

on who has the courage to attack first. If you made a good opening, you may be the one to start the battle.

**The end game** is what the final stage of the game is called. This is the phase when many pieces have already been taken off the board. A skillful player can bring a lot of pressure onto his opponent even with just a few pieces left.

# 10. Don't forget these simple rules

**If you break any of the rules of chess, you may lose the game.** Here are the most important ones:
- Once you touch a piece, you have to move it! When you are thinking about your next move, do not touch your pieces! Once you do this, you will have to move it, even if that means it's a bad decision.
- All beginners should remember that there is no way to reverse a bad move. In chess, nothing can be taken back.
- If you make an illegal move, your piece will be returned to exactly where it was before that move. And if you make a second illegal move, then you simply lose the game.

Please remember that in the game of chess, we need to be polite at all times. This is an absolute must for every real chess player. Good luck in the game!

# 11. Want to be a chess grandmaster? Start playing when you're a kid!

Today, in more than 100 countries around the world, chess is recognized as a sport. Chess players are always trying to improve their ratings and win titles at dedicated competitions. The first international tournament was held in London in the year 1851.

A chess tournament is a series of games that can be won by either one player or an entire team. Wilhelm Steinitz became the first official world chess champion in 1886.

Chess tournaments are graded by the ratings of their participants. The higher the ratings of the tournament's players, the more prestigious the tournament.

In terms of super-high ratings, the Zurich Chess Challenge 2014, held in Zurich, Switzerland, was the first 23$^{rd}$-category tournament in the history of chess.

And the most important team tournament is the Chess Olympiad. Just like in the Olympic Games, all participants of the event represent their nations.

The highest chess title anyone can earn is Grandmaster. Awarded by FIDE for outstanding performance, the title is held for life.

All famous grandmasters of the world began playing chess at a very young age. There are numerous stories about chess prodigies, young children, who could defeat adult masters. For example, at the age of 12, American Paul Morphy defeated a famous European chess master. And only two days before his 13th birthday, José Raúl Capablanca beat the reigning chess champion of Cuba. Most likely the youngest player who competed in serious tournaments was American chess player Samuel Reshevsky, who could play several chess games at once when he was only six years old.

# 12. Chess even has a few relatives around the world

There are around 30 varieties of this ancient game. Though not as popular as traditional chess, they also have their fans. Let's take a quick look at some of them.

**Circular chess** is a chess variant played by classical rules, but on a circular chessboard. There are four rings of squares, sixteen on each. The game was invented by David Reynolds. World championships in circular chess have been held in England since the year 1996.

**Chinese chess, or Xiangqi.** The game is played on a rectangular board of 9 files by 10 ranks. In the center there is a river that can be crossed only by some pieces. Each player has one general, two advisors, elephants, horses, chariots, cannons, and five soldiers. This type of chess is three and a half thousand years old, and today it is played by around 500 million people.

**Japanese chess** is called *shogi*. The battles are played on a board of nine ranks by nine files. Every player has one king, one rook, one bishop, four generals (two silver and two gold),

knights, and lances, as well as nine pawns. All the pieces look almost the same: flat, wedge-shaped, and pentagon-shaped. The way that players tell the pieces apart is by the names written on them in Japanese. *Shogi* is played by around 20 million people all around the world.

# 13. Playing chess in outer space? That's right!

Chess and space. Maybe you are wondering what the two have in common? Well, today's technologies can make the impossible actually possible. In the year 1970, a real space-to-Earth chess match was held! The battle took place between the two cosmonauts aboard the Soyuz 9 spacecraft and "representatives of Earth" down at the mission's ground control center.

The game lasted for around six hours and ended in a draw. During this time, the spacecraft circled the Earth four times. To play the game during conditions of weightlessness, a special zero-gravity chess set was designed. The pieces were attached to the board with special springs. Today, the chessboard and the pieces are on display at the Chess Museum in Moscow.

And in the year 2020, to celebrate the 50th anniversary of the first space-to-Earth chess match, a game was played between a crew member of the International Space Station and a grandmaster down on Earth. It also ended in a draw.

# 14. What about playing chess underwater?

When one chess player was bored with the usual way of playing chess on a table, he dreamed up a new way of playing the game. And so the idea came to him, why not play it underwater? That player was American Etan Ilfeld, and this happened in the year 2011. And then, the very next year, the first world championship in diving chess took place.

The chess match actually takes place in a pool. No special gear is required, just a regular swimsuit. The players take turns diving down and making a move on a chessboard underwater. To keep them from floating, the pieces are held to the board with magnets.

One game lasts for around forty minutes. The championship has four rounds. The rules are the same as those for regular chess. The only requirement is that the players need to decide their moves while they are submerged. Returning to the surface before making a move is not allowed. If you break this one rule, you lose the game. So, if you can hold your breath for long enough underwater, you could possibly win, even if your opponent plays better chess than you. This is how an intellectual game turned into a test of physical endurance.

But a swimming pool is not the only watery place where you can play a game of diving chess. Much to the surprise of sea creatures, some scuba divers are playing chess way down on the ocean floor.

# 15. Welcome to Chess Village, where kids can be game pieces!

Back in the 15th century, a few creative chess players decided to make a chessboard as big as a city square, replace the pieces with actors... and breathe new life into the game! In France and Italy, such "live chess" tournaments were a popular kind of entertainment. A captured "piece" had to bow to the winner and quickly leave the battlefield.

Even nowadays, you can watch "live chess" being played. In Germany, there is a "chess village" where chess is part of the school curriculum and adults are true fans of the game. In the village's coat of arms, there is a chessboard with a knight and a pawn. Famous grandmasters often visit this place and sign the visitors' book. The tradition of playing "live chess" has been going strong there for 300 years. Young people dress up like bishops, knights, rooks, kings, and pawns, and then act out a game of chess.

Every two years, a chess performance is also held in the Italian town of Marostica. It all began with a romantic story that happened more than 500 years ago. Two young knights

challenged each other to a duel to win the heart of a beautiful girl named Lionora, the daughter of their boss, Lord Parisio.

Since both of these young men were very important to Lord Parisio, he didn't want either to die, and so he announced that their fight would take place not with swords or other weapons, but rather on a chessboard.

The game was played in the open air, with the help of the local people. The winner of the match went on to marry the beautiful Lionora, and the loser married Lord Parisio's sister, Oldrada. Everyone lived happily ever after, and the delighted Lord Parisio ordered for the game to be played on the main square for centuries to come.

# 16. Making chess part of your life: for fun, family, and a sharper mind

Chess is a wonderful game for all, wherever you are! You can play it with your family at home, onboard a plane or a train, even on a picnic or in a hotel. With chess, you will never be bored, because every new game is different. There are more game possibilities in chess than there are atoms in the Universe!

Chess brings people together. You can play the game with family, friends, and it can even help you make new friends. You can compete in teams. And you can play chess on the phone, online, or if you are patient enough, by mail.

Even you have no friend to play with, you can still enjoy your favorite game. You can play against a computer. A portable chess set can provide you with hours of fun at home or on a trip. Even just one game will clear your mind and make you feel better!

Every game of chess is a fascinating puzzle to be solved. Chess teaches you not to make impulsive decisions, but instead to think about all the pros and cons of each possible move. This is how we should make the most important choices in life, if we want to succeed. For some people, chess is just a fun activity for their free time. But for others, it is a way of life that builds their motivation to win, and their focus, while refining their character. Learn, practice, and play this amazing game!

# 17. World Chess Champions

Wilhelm Steinitz – Austria-Hungary, USA
Emanuel Lasker – Germany
Jose Raul Capablanca – Cuba, Spain
Alexander Alekhine – Russian Empire, RSFSR, France
Max Euwe – Netherlands
Mikhail Botvinnik – USSR
Vasily Smyslov – USSR, Russian Federation
Mikhail Tal – USSR, Latvia
Tigran Petrosian – USSR
Boris Spassky – USSR, France, Russian Federation
Bobby Fisher – USA, Iceland
Anatoly Karpov – USSR, Russian Federation
Garry Kasparov – USSR, Russian Federation, Croatia
Vladimir Kramnik – USSR, Russian Federation
Viswanathan Anand – India
Magnus Carlsen – Norway

# 18. About the Authors

The wisest, kindest, and smartest books in my life are those written for children. Since I have been helping my husband for many years to organize and manage one of the most famous chess tournaments, the Zurich Chess Challenge, the idea of writing a chess book for children is no accident.

My book with Matthew is the BEGINNING OF THE STORY. For little (and not so little) people, this book opens the door to an unforgettable story full of secrets, legends, and enigmas, a story spanning millennia, the story of a game that has quietly and ingeniously conquered the world.

– Natalie Shevando

**Matthew McMillion** was born in California, just a short walk from the sparkling blue Pacific Ocean. He grew up close to Silicon Valley, in the Santa Cruz Mountains. As a boy, when he wasn't out curiously exploring the forests with his loyal golden retriever, he was often reading books and learning to play games of all kinds. Today, Matthew is a writer and editor in Luxembourg – a land of ancient castles and mysterious legends.

www.ingramcontent.com/pod-product-compliance
Lightning Source LLC
Chambersburg PA
CBHW041506220426
43661CB00016B/1261